50 Quick Bites: Fast and Tasty Snacks

By: Kelly Johnson

Table of Contents

- Mini Caprese Skewers
- Garlic Parmesan Popcorn
- Avocado Toast Bites
- Spicy Chickpea Snack
- Cheese and Cracker Stacks
- Greek Yogurt Dip with Veggies
- Mini Quesadillas
- Peanut Butter Apple Slices
- Hummus and Pita Chips
- Deviled Eggs
- Banana Oat Energy Bites
- Mini Pizza Bagels
- Roasted Almonds
- Fruit and Nut Mix
- Cucumber Sandwiches
- Sweet Potato Chips
- Mozzarella Sticks
- Rice Cake with Nut Butter
- Chocolate-Covered Pretzels
- Baked Zucchini Fries
- Prosciutto-Wrapped Melon
- Mini Tacos
- Egg Salad on Crackers
- Trail Mix
- Roasted Edamame
- Caprese Salad Bites
- Peanut Butter Banana Bites
- Mini Sliders
- Crispy Kale Chips
- Cheese and Apple Slices
- Turkey and Cheese Roll-Ups
- Stuffed Bell Peppers
- Popcorn with Nutritional Yeast
- Tuna Salad on Cucumber Slices
- Yogurt and Granola Parfaits

- Chocolate-Covered Strawberries
- Baked Brie with Crackers
- Guacamole and Tortilla Chips
- Shrimp Cocktail
- Salami and Cheese Roll-Ups
- Roasted Garlic Mushrooms
- Vegetable Spring Rolls
- Baked Sweet Potato Wedges
- Chia Seed Pudding
- Peanut Butter Chocolate Chip Bars
- Air-Fried Cauliflower Bites
- Blueberry and Almond Butter Sandwich
- Pita Bread Pizza
- Hard-Boiled Eggs
- Cucumber Hummus Bites

Mini Caprese Skewers

Ingredients:

- 1 cup cherry tomatoes, halved
- 1 cup mozzarella balls (bocconcini)
- Fresh basil leaves
- 2 tablespoons balsamic glaze
- 1 tablespoon olive oil
- Salt and pepper to taste
- Toothpicks or small skewers

Instructions:

1. **Prepare Ingredients:** Wash and halve the cherry tomatoes. Drain the mozzarella balls if needed.
2. **Assemble Skewers:** Take a toothpick or small skewer and thread a basil leaf, a mozzarella ball, and a cherry tomato half. Repeat until all ingredients are used.
3. **Season:** Drizzle olive oil over the skewers and sprinkle with salt and pepper to taste.
4. **Add Balsamic Glaze:** Drizzle the balsamic glaze over the skewers for a sweet and tangy finish.
5. **Serve:** Arrange the skewers on a platter and serve immediately as a fresh appetizer or snack.

Garlic Parmesan Popcorn
Ingredients:

- 1/2 cup popcorn kernels (or 1 bag of microwave popcorn)
- 2 tablespoons unsalted butter, melted
- 1/4 cup grated Parmesan cheese
- 1 teaspoon garlic powder
- Salt to taste

Instructions:

1. Pop the popcorn kernels in a popcorn maker or microwave.
2. Drizzle the melted butter over the popcorn.
3. Sprinkle with Parmesan cheese, garlic powder, and salt.
4. Toss to coat evenly and serve.

Avocado Toast Bites

Ingredients:

- 1 ripe avocado, mashed
- 1/2 teaspoon lemon juice
- Salt and pepper to taste
- 1 baguette, sliced into small rounds
- Olive oil for toasting

Instructions:

1. Preheat the oven to 375°F (190°C).
2. Lightly brush the baguette slices with olive oil and toast them in the oven until golden.
3. Mix mashed avocado with lemon juice, salt, and pepper.
4. Spread the avocado mixture onto the toasted baguette rounds and serve.

Spicy Chickpea Snack
Ingredients:

- 1 can (15 oz) chickpeas, drained and rinsed
- 1 tablespoon olive oil
- 1 teaspoon smoked paprika
- 1/2 teaspoon chili powder
- Salt to taste

Instructions:

1. Preheat the oven to 400°F (200°C).
2. Pat the chickpeas dry with a paper towel and toss them with olive oil and spices.
3. Spread them in a single layer on a baking sheet.
4. Roast for 25-30 minutes, shaking the pan halfway through.
5. Let them cool before serving.

Cheese and Cracker Stacks
Ingredients:

- Assorted crackers (e.g., Ritz, wheat crackers)
- Your choice of cheese (cheddar, brie, gouda, etc.), sliced
- Fresh herbs (optional), like basil or rosemary

Instructions:

1. Lay a cracker on a plate and top it with a slice of cheese.
2. Add another cracker on top and repeat until you have your desired stack height.
3. Garnish with fresh herbs for an extra touch and serve.

Greek Yogurt Dip with Veggies
Ingredients:

- 1 cup plain Greek yogurt
- 1 tablespoon olive oil
- 1 tablespoon lemon juice
- 1 garlic clove, minced
- 1 teaspoon dried dill
- Salt and pepper to taste
- Fresh vegetables (carrot sticks, cucumber slices, bell pepper strips)

Instructions:

1. In a bowl, combine Greek yogurt, olive oil, lemon juice, garlic, dill, salt, and pepper.
2. Mix until smooth and creamy.
3. Serve with fresh vegetable sticks for dipping.

Mini Quesadillas
Ingredients:

- 4 small flour tortillas
- 1 cup shredded cheddar cheese
- 1/2 cup cooked chicken (optional), diced
- 1/4 cup diced bell pepper
- 1/4 cup diced onion
- Olive oil for cooking

Instructions:

1. Heat a skillet over medium heat and lightly brush with olive oil.
2. Place one tortilla in the pan and sprinkle with cheese, chicken, bell pepper, and onion.
3. Top with another tortilla and cook until golden on both sides, flipping once.
4. Slice into wedges and serve.

Peanut Butter Apple Slices
Ingredients:

- 2 apples, cored and sliced
- 1/4 cup peanut butter
- 1 tablespoon honey (optional)
- Chopped nuts or granola for topping (optional)

Instructions:

1. Arrange apple slices on a plate.
2. Drizzle peanut butter over each slice and add a little honey if desired.
3. Top with chopped nuts or granola for added crunch.

Hummus and Pita Chips
Ingredients:

- 1 cup hummus (store-bought or homemade)
- 1 pack pita chips

Instructions:

1. Serve hummus in a bowl alongside a dish of pita chips.
2. Enjoy as a quick and healthy dip.

Deviled Eggs
Ingredients:

- 6 hard-boiled eggs
- 3 tablespoons mayonnaise
- 1 teaspoon mustard
- 1 tablespoon vinegar
- Paprika for garnish
- Salt and pepper to taste

Instructions:

1. Slice hard-boiled eggs in half and remove the yolks.
2. Mash the yolks with mayonnaise, mustard, vinegar, salt, and pepper.
3. Spoon the mixture back into the egg whites and garnish with paprika.

Banana Oat Energy Bites
Ingredients:

- 1 ripe banana, mashed
- 1 cup rolled oats
- 1/4 cup peanut butter
- 1/4 cup chocolate chips (optional)
- 1 tablespoon honey
- 1/2 teaspoon vanilla extract

Instructions:

1. In a bowl, mix all ingredients until well combined.
2. Roll the mixture into small balls.
3. Refrigerate for at least 30 minutes before serving.

Mini Pizza Bagels
Ingredients:

- 6 mini bagels, halved
- 1/2 cup pizza sauce
- 1 cup shredded mozzarella cheese
- 1/4 cup pepperoni or veggies (optional)

Instructions:

1. Preheat oven to 375°F (190°C).
2. Spread pizza sauce on each bagel half.
3. Top with mozzarella cheese and optional toppings.
4. Bake for 8-10 minutes until cheese is melted.

Roasted Almonds
Ingredients:

- 1 cup raw almonds
- 1 tablespoon olive oil
- 1/2 teaspoon sea salt

Instructions:

1. Preheat oven to 350°F (175°C).
2. Toss almonds in olive oil and sea salt.
3. Spread them on a baking sheet and roast for 10-12 minutes, stirring halfway through.

Fruit and Nut Mix
Ingredients:

- 1/2 cup dried cranberries
- 1/2 cup mixed nuts (almonds, cashews, walnuts)
- 1/2 cup dark chocolate chips
- 1/2 cup dried apricots, chopped

Instructions:

1. In a bowl, combine all ingredients and mix well.
2. Store in an airtight container and serve as a snack.

Cucumber Sandwiches
Ingredients:

- 1 cucumber, thinly sliced
- 8 slices whole grain bread
- 4 ounces cream cheese
- Fresh dill or parsley for garnish

Instructions:

1. Spread cream cheese on each slice of bread.
2. Layer cucumber slices on half of the bread slices.
3. Top with the remaining bread slices and garnish with fresh herbs.
4. Slice into halves or quarters and serve.

Sweet Potato Chips
Ingredients:

- 2 large sweet potatoes, thinly sliced
- 1 tablespoon olive oil
- Salt to taste
- Pepper to taste

Instructions:

1. Preheat oven to 400°F (200°C).
2. Toss sweet potato slices in olive oil, salt, and pepper.
3. Spread evenly on a baking sheet.
4. Bake for 20-25 minutes, flipping halfway through, until crispy.

Mozzarella Sticks
Ingredients:

- 12 mozzarella sticks (store-bought or homemade)
- 1/2 cup all-purpose flour
- 2 large eggs, beaten
- 1 cup breadcrumbs
- 1 teaspoon dried oregano
- 1/2 teaspoon garlic powder
- Olive oil for frying

Instructions:

1. Dip mozzarella sticks in flour, then egg, and finally coat with breadcrumbs mixed with oregano and garlic powder.
2. Heat olive oil in a pan over medium heat and fry mozzarella sticks until golden brown and crispy.
3. Drain on paper towels and serve with marinara sauce.

Rice Cake with Nut Butter
Ingredients:

- 2 rice cakes
- 2 tablespoons almond butter or peanut butter
- Sliced banana or strawberries (optional)
- A drizzle of honey (optional)

Instructions:

1. Spread nut butter evenly over the rice cakes.
2. Top with sliced banana or strawberries and drizzle with honey if desired.
3. Serve as a quick snack.

Chocolate-Covered Pretzels
Ingredients:

- 1 cup mini pretzels
- 1 cup dark or milk chocolate chips
- 1 tablespoon coconut oil (optional, for smoother chocolate)

Instructions:

1. Melt chocolate chips with coconut oil (if using) in a microwave or over a double boiler.
2. Dip pretzels into the melted chocolate, coating them halfway.
3. Place on parchment paper and let the chocolate set.
4. Enjoy after the chocolate hardens.

Baked Zucchini Fries
Ingredients:

- 2 medium zucchinis, sliced into fries
- 1/2 cup breadcrumbs
- 1/4 cup grated Parmesan cheese
- 1 teaspoon garlic powder
- Salt and pepper to taste
- 1 egg, beaten

Instructions:

1. Preheat oven to 425°F (220°C).
2. Toss zucchini fries in egg, then coat in breadcrumb and Parmesan mixture.
3. Spread on a baking sheet and bake for 20-25 minutes, flipping halfway through.
4. Serve with marinara or ranch dip.

Prosciutto-Wrapped Melon

Ingredients:

- 1 small melon (cantaloupe or honeydew), cut into cubes
- 6 slices prosciutto, cut in half
- Fresh mint leaves (optional)

Instructions:

1. Wrap a slice of prosciutto around each melon cube.
2. Secure with a toothpick and garnish with fresh mint if desired.
3. Serve chilled.

Mini Tacos
Ingredients:

- 6 small soft corn tortillas
- 1 cup cooked ground beef or chicken
- 1/4 cup shredded cheese
- Salsa, sour cream, and guacamole for topping

Instructions:

1. Warm tortillas in a pan or microwave.
2. Fill each tortilla with ground meat, cheese, salsa, sour cream, and guacamole.
3. Fold into mini tacos and serve.

Egg Salad on Crackers
Ingredients:

- 4 hard-boiled eggs, chopped
- 2 tablespoons mayonnaise
- 1 teaspoon mustard
- Salt and pepper to taste
- Assorted crackers

Instructions:

1. Mix chopped eggs, mayonnaise, mustard, salt, and pepper in a bowl.
2. Spoon the egg salad onto crackers and serve.

Trail Mix
Ingredients:

- 1 cup mixed nuts (almonds, cashews, walnuts)
- 1/2 cup dried fruit (cranberries, raisins, apricots)
- 1/4 cup chocolate chips or M&Ms
- 1/4 cup sunflower seeds or pumpkin seeds

Instructions:

1. Combine all ingredients in a large bowl.
2. Store in an airtight container and serve as a snack.

Roasted Edamame

Ingredients:

- 2 cups frozen edamame, thawed
- 1 tablespoon olive oil
- 1/2 teaspoon sea salt
- 1/2 teaspoon garlic powder

Instructions:

1. Preheat oven to 400°F (200°C).
2. Toss edamame in olive oil, salt, and garlic powder.
3. Spread on a baking sheet and roast for 15-20 minutes, shaking halfway through.

Caprese Salad Bites
Ingredients:

- 1 cup cherry tomatoes, halved
- 1 cup mozzarella balls (bocconcini)
- Fresh basil leaves
- Balsamic glaze for drizzling

Instructions:

1. Thread a basil leaf, mozzarella ball, and tomato half onto a toothpick.
2. Drizzle with balsamic glaze and serve.

Peanut Butter Banana Bites
Ingredients:

- 1 ripe banana, sliced
- 1/4 cup peanut butter
- 1/4 cup granola or chopped nuts

Instructions:

1. Spread peanut butter on each banana slice.
2. Top with granola or chopped nuts for extra crunch.
3. Serve immediately as a snack.

Mini Sliders
Ingredients:

- 12 slider buns
- 1 lb ground beef or turkey
- 1/2 teaspoon garlic powder
- 1/2 teaspoon onion powder
- Salt and pepper to taste
- Cheese slices (optional)
- Lettuce, tomato, pickles for toppings

Instructions:

1. Form ground meat into 12 small patties and season with garlic powder, onion powder, salt, and pepper.
2. Cook the patties in a skillet or on a grill until fully cooked.
3. Assemble sliders by placing the patties on buns and adding cheese, lettuce, tomato, and pickles.

Crispy Kale Chips
Ingredients:

- 1 bunch kale, washed and torn into pieces
- 1 tablespoon olive oil
- Salt to taste
- 1/4 teaspoon garlic powder

Instructions:

1. Preheat oven to 375°F (190°C).
2. Toss kale pieces with olive oil, salt, and garlic powder.
3. Spread in a single layer on a baking sheet and bake for 10-15 minutes, until crispy.

Cheese and Apple Slices
Ingredients:

- 1 apple, sliced
- 1/2 cup cheese (cheddar, brie, or gouda), sliced
- Honey for drizzling (optional)

Instructions:

1. Arrange apple slices and cheese slices on a platter.
2. Drizzle with honey if desired and serve as a refreshing snack.

Turkey and Cheese Roll-Ups
Ingredients:

- 8 slices deli turkey
- 4 slices cheese (cheddar, Swiss, or provolone)
- Fresh spinach or lettuce (optional)

Instructions:

1. Lay a slice of cheese on top of each slice of turkey.
2. Add spinach or lettuce if desired.
3. Roll up each slice of turkey and cheese and serve as a quick snack.

Stuffed Bell Peppers
Ingredients:

- 4 mini bell peppers, halved and seeded
- 1/2 cup cooked quinoa or rice
- 1/2 cup black beans, drained and rinsed
- 1/4 cup shredded cheese
- 1/4 teaspoon cumin

Instructions:

1. Preheat oven to 375°F (190°C).
2. Mix quinoa or rice, black beans, cheese, and cumin in a bowl.
3. Stuff the mini bell peppers with the mixture and bake for 15-20 minutes, until peppers are tender.

Popcorn with Nutritional Yeast
Ingredients:

- 1/2 cup popcorn kernels (or 1 bag microwave popcorn)
- 2 tablespoons nutritional yeast
- 1 tablespoon olive oil
- Salt to taste

Instructions:

1. Pop the popcorn kernels.
2. Drizzle with olive oil and sprinkle with nutritional yeast and salt.
3. Toss to coat evenly and serve.

Tuna Salad on Cucumber Slices
Ingredients:

- 1 can tuna, drained
- 2 tablespoons mayonnaise
- 1 teaspoon Dijon mustard
- Salt and pepper to taste
- 1 cucumber, sliced

Instructions:

1. Mix tuna, mayonnaise, Dijon mustard, salt, and pepper in a bowl.
2. Spoon the tuna salad onto cucumber slices and serve as a refreshing snack.

Yogurt and Granola Parfaits
Ingredients:

- 1 cup plain Greek yogurt
- 1/4 cup granola
- 1/2 cup mixed berries (strawberries, blueberries, raspberries)
- Honey for drizzling (optional)

Instructions:

1. Layer yogurt, granola, and berries in small glasses or bowls.
2. Drizzle with honey if desired and serve chilled.

Chocolate-Covered Strawberries
Ingredients:

- 12 strawberries, washed and dried
- 1/2 cup dark or milk chocolate chips
- 1 tablespoon coconut oil (optional)

Instructions:

1. Melt chocolate chips with coconut oil in a microwave or over a double boiler.
2. Dip each strawberry into the melted chocolate and place on parchment paper to set.
3. Let the chocolate harden and serve.

Baked Brie with Crackers
Ingredients:

- 1 wheel of brie cheese
- 2 tablespoons honey
- 1/4 cup chopped nuts (walnuts or pecans)
- Assorted crackers for serving

Instructions:

1. Preheat oven to 350°F (175°C).
2. Place the brie on a baking sheet and bake for 10-12 minutes until soft.
3. Drizzle with honey and sprinkle with chopped nuts.
4. Serve with crackers.

Guacamole and Tortilla Chips
Ingredients:

- 2 ripe avocados, mashed
- 1/2 small onion, finely chopped
- 1 tomato, diced
- 1 tablespoon lime juice
- Salt and pepper to taste
- Tortilla chips for serving

Instructions:

1. Mash the avocados and mix with onion, tomato, lime juice, salt, and pepper.
2. Serve with tortilla chips for dipping.

Shrimp Cocktail
Ingredients:

- 12 large shrimp, peeled and deveined
- 1 tablespoon olive oil
- Salt and pepper to taste
- 1/2 cup cocktail sauce
- Lemon wedges for serving

Instructions:

1. Preheat oven to 400°F (200°C).
2. Toss shrimp with olive oil, salt, and pepper.
3. Arrange shrimp on a baking sheet and roast for 8-10 minutes, until cooked through.
4. Serve with cocktail sauce and lemon wedges.

Salami and Cheese Roll-Ups
Ingredients:

- 8 slices of salami
- 8 slices of cheese (cheddar, Swiss, or provolone)
- Fresh herbs for garnish (optional)

Instructions:

1. Lay a slice of cheese on each slice of salami.
2. Roll them up tightly and secure with a toothpick.
3. Garnish with fresh herbs and serve.

Roasted Garlic Mushrooms

Ingredients:

- 1 lb mushrooms, cleaned and trimmed
- 2 tablespoons olive oil
- 4 cloves garlic, minced
- Salt and pepper to taste
- Fresh parsley for garnish

Instructions:

1. Preheat oven to 375°F (190°C).
2. Toss mushrooms with olive oil, garlic, salt, and pepper.
3. Roast for 20-25 minutes, stirring occasionally.
4. Garnish with parsley and serve.

Vegetable Spring Rolls
Ingredients:

- 8 spring roll wrappers
- 1/2 cup shredded carrots
- 1/2 cup cucumber, julienned
- 1/2 cup bell pepper, thinly sliced
- Fresh cilantro and mint leaves
- Rice paper for wrapping
- Dipping sauce (optional)

Instructions:

1. Soak the spring roll wrappers in warm water for about 20 seconds.
2. Layer vegetables and herbs on the wrapper.
3. Roll tightly and cut in half.
4. Serve with a dipping sauce of choice.

Baked Sweet Potato Wedges

Ingredients:

- 2 medium sweet potatoes, cut into wedges
- 1 tablespoon olive oil
- 1 teaspoon smoked paprika
- Salt and pepper to taste

Instructions:

1. Preheat oven to 425°F (220°C).
2. Toss sweet potato wedges with olive oil, smoked paprika, salt, and pepper.
3. Spread in a single layer on a baking sheet and bake for 25-30 minutes, until crispy.

Chia Seed Pudding
Ingredients:

- 2 tablespoons chia seeds
- 1 cup almond milk (or other milk of choice)
- 1 tablespoon maple syrup or honey
- Fresh berries or fruit for topping

Instructions:

1. Mix chia seeds, almond milk, and maple syrup in a bowl.
2. Refrigerate for at least 2 hours or overnight to thicken.
3. Top with fresh berries or fruit before serving.

Peanut Butter Chocolate Chip Bars

Ingredients:

- 1 cup peanut butter
- 1/2 cup honey or maple syrup
- 1 cup rolled oats
- 1/2 cup chocolate chips

Instructions:

1. Preheat oven to 350°F (175°C).
2. Mix peanut butter, honey, oats, and chocolate chips in a bowl.
3. Press into a baking dish and bake for 15-18 minutes.
4. Cool, cut into bars, and serve.

Air-Fried Cauliflower Bites
Ingredients:

- 1 medium cauliflower, cut into florets
- 2 tablespoons olive oil
- 1/2 teaspoon paprika
- Salt and pepper to taste

Instructions:

1. Preheat the air fryer to 375°F (190°C).
2. Toss cauliflower florets with olive oil, paprika, salt, and pepper.
3. Air fry for 15-20 minutes, shaking the basket halfway through.
4. Serve warm.

Blueberry and Almond Butter Sandwich
Ingredients:

- 2 slices whole-grain bread
- 2 tablespoons almond butter
- 1/4 cup fresh blueberries

Instructions:

1. Spread almond butter on one slice of bread.
2. Top with fresh blueberries and place the second slice of bread on top.
3. Serve as a quick snack.

Pita Bread Pizza
Ingredients:

- 1 pita bread
- 1/4 cup pizza sauce
- 1/2 cup shredded mozzarella cheese
- 1/4 cup pepperoni or vegetables for topping (optional)

Instructions:

1. Preheat oven to 375°F (190°C).
2. Spread pizza sauce on the pita bread.
3. Sprinkle with mozzarella cheese and top with your choice of toppings.
4. Bake for 8-10 minutes, until the cheese is melted.

Hard-Boiled Eggs
Ingredients:

- 6 eggs

Instructions:

1. Place eggs in a saucepan and cover with cold water.
2. Bring to a boil and then reduce heat to low.
3. Simmer for 10 minutes, then remove from heat and cool under cold running water.
4. Peel and serve.

Cucumber Hummus Bites
Ingredients:

- 1 cucumber, sliced
- 1/2 cup hummus
- Fresh dill for garnish (optional)

Instructions:

1. Slice cucumber into thick rounds.
2. Spoon hummus onto each cucumber slice.
3. Garnish with fresh dill and serve.

www.ingramcontent.com/pod-product-compliance
Lightning Source LLC
LaVergne TN
LVHW061956070526
838199LV00060B/4152